60-Day Prayer Map

by

Vivian Ojieh

60-Day Prayer Map

by

Vivian Ojieh

Copyright © 2021

ISBN 978-1-7366116-0-9

Second Edition

Dedication

I would like to dedicate this book to my Lord who inspires me by the Holy Spirit. I also dedicate this book and series to my husband and partner Hesed, who pushed and challenged me to begin this journey, and to my beloved children, Chidinma, Chinwe, and Isaac who all cheer me to be the best version of myself.

Acknowledgements

I am grateful to the members of Wealthy Creek TDC, this book is a compilation of the daily morning prayers that I started to write because of you. Thank you all for inspiring me to begin the Prayer Map Series.

Preface

This is the second edition of *60-Day Prayer Map*. I have always enjoyed making prayer points from Bible verses and this book is a collection of 60 days of early morning prayer points. *60-Day Prayer Map* aims to assist readers in their daily devotions. Each daily prayer consists of a relevant scripture broken down into a couple or more prayer points. It may be most helpful to say the prayers aloud and allow oneself to flow naturally into more focused prayers as the Holy Spirit leads.

Day 1

"For it is God who works in you, both to will and to work for his good pleasure."
— Philippians 2:13, NIV

O Lord, I yield myself to the working of Your spirit, activate in me both the desire and the ability to do Your will, in Jesus' name.

O Lord open my eyes to an opportunity to work for Your pleasure today, in Jesus' name, amen!

Day 2

"But the anointing which you have received from Him abides in you, and you do not need that anyone teach you; but as the same anointing teaches you concerning all things, and is true, and is not a lie, and just as it has taught you, you will abide in Him". — 1 John 2:27

O Lord, I thank You for Your anointing which is on me, teach me, by the same anointing, every deep secret to overcome any demonic obstacle in my path today.

Enable me to stay in the anointing and abide in You today, in Jesus' mighty name, amen!

Day 3

"Of sons of Issachar who had understanding of the times, to know what Israel ought to do, their chiefs were two hundred; and all their brethren were at their command."
— 1 Chronicles 12:32

O Lord, I thank You for granting me a new opportunity to fulfill my divine destiny. Show me what to do right now and in the days to come.

Like the Sons of Issachar, anoint me to understand the times and seasons of my life, help me see and hear what You are doing with, around, and through my life today, in Jesus' mighty name, amen!

Day 4

"Some Gadites joined David at the stronghold in the wilderness, mighty men of valor, men trained for battle, who could handle shield and spear, whose faces were like the faces of lions, and were as swift as gazelles on the mountains." — 1 Chronicles 12:8

O Lord, I thank You for granting me a new day in Your presence.

By Your Holy Spirit, train my hands for spiritual warfare, grant me speed in all I do, help me recover every lost time and opportunity, by Your grace and favor.

Strengthen me to face every situation with boldness and courage, in Jesus' mighty name, amen!

Day 5

"See, I have this day set you over the nations and over the kingdoms, To root out and to pull down, To destroy and to throw down, To build and to plant." – Jeremiah 1:10

Thank You, Lord, for the authority to dismantle and rebuild foundations concerning my life.

By Your Holy Spirit, open my eyes to any faulty foundation in my life.

By the authority of the Word of God, I pull down and uproot every faulty foundation in my prayer life, in my marriage, in my health, in my relationships, in my business, in my job, and in my education, in Jesus' mighty name, amen!

I plant and establish divine order in my prayer life (repeat prayer for any other faulty foundation), in Jesus' mighty name, amen.

Day 6

"Let the words of my mouth and the meditation of my heart Be acceptable in your sight, O LORD, my strength and my Redeemer."
— Psalm 19:14

Thank You, O Lord, for Your grace and mercy upon my life today.

I commit my heart and lips to You Lord, purify them, O Lord.

Help me think positively instead of negatively. May I think on things that are pure, uplifting, joyful, and spirit-building.

I come against every depressing thought of hatred, failure, and death, in Jesus' name.

May my lips speak words of life, peace, hope, love, and growth, in Jesus' name, amen.

Day 7

"These things I have spoken to you, that in Me you may have peace. In the world, you will have tribulation; but be of good cheer, I have overcome the world." – John 16:33

Thank You Father, for Your steadfast love that never ceases and for Your peace which defies human understanding.

By the authority of Your Word, I refuse every worry and anxiety.

By Your anointing, strengthen me to face and triumph over any tribulation, trial, circumstance, or situation with boldness and confidence because You have overcome the world.

I declare in the name of Jesus, that I am an overcomer and I will continue to be of good cheer, in the mighty name of Jesus, amen.

Notes

Day 8

"Knowing this, that our old man was crucified with Him, that the body of sin might be done away with, that we should no longer be slaves of sin." – Romans 6:6

I worship You, Lord, for this new day, thank You for Your Word by which I have the authority to die to sin and be alive to God.

In the name of Jesus Christ my savior, I declare my freedom from any attraction or connection to sin because my old man was crucified with Christ.

I break every chain of sin and unrighteousness from my life, I disconnect myself from every sinful habit and addiction (name the sinful habits and/or addictions).

Holy Spirit, strengthen me to stay in the anointing (in close fellowship with You). Beginning today, I am no longer a slave to sin, in Jesus' mighty name, amen.

Day 9

"Worship the Lord your God, and his blessing will be on your food and water. I will take away sickness from among you." – Exodus 23:25, NIV

I worship You Lord, the glory and the lifter of my head. Thank You for Your new mercies upon my life every day.

By Your anointing, stir in me the spirit of a true worshipper, may my praises be a sweet sacrifice, holy and acceptable to You today.

As I worship You, may Your blessings be upon all food and water I consume today, that it may be a source of nourishment to me and not a cause for disease, in Jesus' name.

By Your power, may any poisonous substance lose its power against my body and be neutralized, in Jesus' name

In the name of Jesus, I break every chain of sickness and infirmity from my life, I disconnect myself from every hereditary disease (mention any known sickness or disease).

I am healed, in Jesus' name, amen.

Day 10

"If my people, who are called by my name, will humble themselves and pray and seek my face and turn from their wicked ways, then I will hear from heaven, and I will forgive their sin and will heal their land."
– 2 Chronicles 7:14, NIV

Thank You, Lord, because You created me and called me perfect, by Your mercy I live to see another day. Father, I worship You.

Today I humble myself before You, I repent of any selfishness in me, of every way I have deviated from Your will and call for my life. I repent of any incomplete obedience to Your word and of every other known sin in my life (mention any that come to your mind and spirit), please forgive me Lord, in Jesus' name.

Lord, I lift this land before You, open my eyes to see the prayer needs of this area. Today I bring my land/city/nation/community before You and ask that You intervene to heal this place.

I come against the spirit of violence, greed, manipulation, hatred, strife, sickness, poverty, etc., in Jesus' mighty name.

Let Your healing power begin to manifest in this land, in Jesus' name. Father raise up intercessors who will have a prayer burden for my community.

Raise godly leaders who will execute Your will and purpose in this land, I pray for Your wisdom and love to guide our leaders, in Jesus' name.

Day 11

"They shall not hurt nor destroy in all My holy mountain, For the earth shall be full of the knowledge of the Lord As the waters cover the sea." – Isaiah 11:9

Thank You Lord for divine protection on Your holy mountain. Thank you for your protection on my church, home and on all other places which have been dedicated to you.

May the knowledge of You and Your holy name spread through our nation and all over the earth in Jesus' mighty name.

May more and more people come to find protection in Your house, in Jesus' name.

Day 12

"For the earth will be filled with the knowledge of the glory of the Lord as the waters cover the sea." – Habakkuk 2:14, NIV

Thank You, almighty God, for another anointed day in my life.

In the mighty name of Jesus, I pray for Your glory to cover my life, home, church, business, workplace, city, and nation. Let there be an increase in the number of people who know and honor You in (mention the location).

I pray for the addition of new souls to Your kingdom today, through the preaching of Your Word, in our church services, on the streets and through diverse ministries, let the hearts of people be touched by Your glory.

As Your glory covers our churches and cities, let Your power and presence subdue every contrary power and presence, in Jesus' name.

Lord, as Your glory covers me today, let the reality of Your power and presence in my life be revealed to me in a new way, in Jesus' mighty name.

Day 13

"But I say, walk by the Spirit, and you will not gratify the desires of the flesh."
– Galatians 5:16, ESV

Thank You, Father, for the beginning of another anointed day in my life.

I pray for divine enablement to keep in step with the Holy Spirit. Lord, help me to be conscious of Your constant presence in my life.

Help me, Holy Spirit, to submit to the Word in all things and to keep away from every appearance of evil, in Jesus' name.

Strengthen me Lord, to stay connected to You, so that Your power and anointing will manifest in my life beginning today, in the mighty name of Jesus, amen!

Day 14

"Depart from here and turn eastward and hide yourself by the brook Cherith, which is east of the Jordan. You shall drink from the brook, and I have commanded the ravens to feed you there."
— 1 Kings 17:3-4, ESV

"Then the word of the Lord came to him, "Arise, go to Zarephath, which belongs to Sidon, and dwell there. Behold, I have commanded a widow there to feed you."
— 1 Kings 17:8-9, ESV

O Lord, I thank You for this day, I worship You and I bless Your holy name.

Holy Spirit, open my eyes and lead me to the location of my divine supply and sustenance.

Order my steps and connect me, by favor, to the person You have appointed to bless me today, in Jesus' name.

The season of drought and lack is broken from my life, in Jesus' mighty name, amen!

Notes

Day 15

"Up, sanctify the people, and say, sanctify yourselves against to morrow: for thus saith the Lord God of Israel, There is an accursed thing in the midst of thee, O Israel: thou canst not stand before thine enemies, until ye take away the accursed thing from among you." – Joshua 7:13, KJV

I worship You, Lord. You are worthy to be praised and adored.

I present myself before You, sanctify me by the blood of the Lamb, purify me by the anointing.

Holy Ghost fire, consume every unclean or cursed thing in my life. Everything that I'm holding on to which is not of God, I release today, in Jesus' name.

Because I am fully submitted and consecrated to You, Lord, I receive the power to withstand every enemy of my destiny, in Jesus' name, amen.

Day 16

"But on Mount Zion will be deliverance; it will be holy, and Jacob will possess his inheritance." – Obadiah 1:17, NIV

Thank You, Lord, for a new day.

In the name of Jesus, standing upon mount Zion, I command every chain of bondage over my finances, my children, my business, my mind, and my prayer life to break right now.

I begin to repossess everything (mention lost possessions which come to mind) Satan has taken away from me, I reclaim my divine allocation and inheritance, in Jesus' mighty name, amen.

Day 17

"Tremble, earth, at the presence of the Lord, at the presence of the God of Jacob."
– Psalm 114:7, NIV

Thank You, Father, for the dawn of a new day.

Lord, I submit myself to You, and separate myself from everything that will take me from Your presence today, in Jesus' name.

Let the power of Your presence manifest in my life today, let every troublesome situation, every obstacle and hindrance in my path tremble and flee because of Your anointing, in the mighty name of Jesus.

Day 18

"Now the Jordan is at flood stage all during harvest. Yet as soon as the priests who carried the ark reached the Jordan and their feet touched the water's edge, the water from upstream stopped flowing. It piled up in a heap a great distance away, at a town called Adam in the vicinity of Zarethan, while the water flowing down to the Sea of the Arabah (that is, the Dead Sea) was completely cut off. So the people crossed over opposite Jericho."
— Joshua 3:15-16, NIV

Thank You, Father, for another day.

As I remain in Your presence today, strengthen me to take my step of faith (ask Him to reveal what step of faith should be taken). I come against every limitation in my way, in Jesus' name.

I call forth open doors of opportunity, mercy, favor, breakthrough, provision, and divine connections because of Your presence in my life, in Jesus' name.

Day 19

"I rejoiced with those who said to me, "Let us go to the house of the Lord."
– Psalm 122:1, NIV

Thank You, Lord, for another day to bask in Your glory. May the zeal of Your house consume me, let my heart fill with joy as I fellowship with Your people.

In the name of Jesus, I come against every hindrance that will stop people from coming into Your house.

I call forth people from every part of the city to rush into the gathering of Your people, in Jesus' mighty name. May Your power and glory manifest among your church, in Jesus' mighty name, amen.

Day 20

"For nothing will be impossible with God." – Luke 1:37, ESV

I thank You, Father of glory, in whom there is no shadow of impossibility, for a new opportunity to shine by grace.

In the mighty name of Jesus, I cast out every fear of impossible situations. I call those things which are not possible (name the impossible situation) into being by the creative power of the almighty God.

I command every blocked door before me to open, by the power of the Holy Spirit, I command every mountain of difficulty before me today to be made plain and every valley to be made level, every crooked path to straighten, in Jesus' name, amen.

Day 21

"Behold, they shall surely gather together, but not by me: whosoever shall gather together against thee shall fall for thy sake." – Isaiah 54:15, KJV

"No weapon that is formed against thee shall prosper; and every tongue that shall rise against thee in judgment thou shalt condemn. This is the heritage of the servants of the Lord, and their righteousness is of me, saith the Lord." – Isaiah 54:17, KJV

I thank You, Lord, for this new day.

By the Holy Ghost anointing and fire, I scatter every unauthorized gathering against me where my name is being mentioned for evil, in Jesus' mighty name. Every attacker shall fall for my sake, in Jesus' name.

I declare, no ungodly, demonic weapon fashioned against me shall prosper and I render all the demonic devices against me today unfruitful, in Jesus' mighty name, amen.

Notes

Day 22

"Hearken unto me, ye that know righteousness, the people in whose heart is my law; fear not the reproach of men, and be not afraid of their revilings." — Isaiah 51:7, KJV

Thank you, Jesus, for Your blood which takes away my sins.

Help me, Lord, to receive Your Word in my heart today and be obedient to Your voice, may I be single-minded in my faith. Let your arm of miracles manifest power in my life today, in Jesus' name.

Holy Spirit, empower me to act according to Your leading and not out of fear of the reproach or insults of man, in Jesus' name, amen.

Day 23

"Finally, brethren, whatever things are true, whatever things are noble, whatever things are just, whatever things are pure, whatever things are lovely, whatever things are of good report, if there is any virtue and if there is anything praiseworthy—meditate on these things." – Philippians 4:8

Thank You Lord, for Your grace and mercy.

I arrest every strange thought and word trying to penetrate my mind, in the mighty name of Jesus, today I will meditate upon things that are true, lovely, pure, of good report, virtuous and praiseworthy. I refuse every unfruitful thought, in Jesus' name.

Let your power manifest in and through my mind to activate Your promises in my life, I reject every failure and disgrace, in Jesus' name, amen.

Day 24

"For I am the Lord. I speak, and the word which I speak will come to pass; it will no more be postponed; for in your days, O rebellious house, I will say the word and perform it," says the Lord God.'" – Ezekiel 12:25

Thank You, Lord, for the power of Your spoken Word.

I repent of every rebellion in my heart and life in Jesus name, I yield myself completely to Your divine purpose.

Father, may Your Word be performed speedily in my life without delay in Jesus name, amen.

Day 25

"For the Lord will comfort Zion, He will comfort all her waste places; He will make her wilderness like Eden, And her desert like the garden of the Lord; Joy and gladness will be found in it, Thanksgiving and the voice of melody." – Isaiah 51:3

In the name of Jesus, I open my heart to receive Your comfort today, O Lord. I speak the Zoe life of God to every barren place, wilderness or desert in or around my life, may my life express freshness like the garden of the Lord, in Jesus' mighty name.

Let the joy and gladness that come from Your throne of grace manifest in my life today and let my lips be filled with praise and thanksgiving instead of heaviness, in Jesus' name I pray, amen.

Day 26

"Hearken unto me, my people; and give ear unto me, O my nation: for a law shall proceed from me, and I will make my judgment to rest for a light of the people." – Isaiah 51:4, KJV

Oh Lord, sharpen my spiritual senses today, in Jesus' mighty name. May I be fully in tune with Your divine revelation, and as I receive Your instruction, help me to obey, in Jesus' name.

I come against every spirit of distraction that causes me not to hear Your Word and instruction as it goes forth. I bind every spirit of deafness from operating in and around me in, Jesus' name.

Let Your judgement manifest against any agent hindering people from receiving the gospel, in Jesus' name.

Day 27

"My righteousness is near; my salvation is gone forth, and mine arms shall judge the people; the isles shall wait upon me, and on mine arm shall they trust." – Isaiah 51:5, KJV

Thank You, Father, for Your mercies which are new to me daily, I put my trust in You today.

According to Your Word, O Lord, let the fulfillment of Your promises begin in my life today (say the promises aloud). I declare the manifestation of the words You have spoken concerning my life, in Jesus' name.

Father, execute Your promise of salvation to those who call upon You, use me as an evangelist in Jesus' name.

Let Your arm execute judgement upon those who stand against the spread of Your gospel, in the mighty name of Jesus.

Day 28

"Awake, awake, put on strength, O arm of the Lord; awake, as in the ancient days, in the generations of old. Art thou not it that hath cut Rahab, and wounded the dragon?"
– Isaiah 51:9, KJV

"And forgettest the Lord thy maker, that hath stretched forth the heavens, and laid the foundations of the earth; and hast feared continually every day because of the fury of the oppressor, as if he were ready to destroy? and where is the fury of the oppressor?"
– Isaiah 51:13, KJV

Thank You, Abba Father, for another day of victory in Your presence.

O Lord who rescued me in the past, extend Your victorious arm of miracles and wage war on my behalf today.

Arise, O Lord, and scatter every enemy of my divine destiny, in the mighty name of Jesus. I take authority over every oppressor standing against the fulfillment of Your plan and purpose for my life.

I come against every fear of oppressors in my life, in Jesus' name. I declare, I have overcome by the blood of the Lamb, amen.

Notes

Day 29

"Therefore hear this, you afflicted one, made drunk, but not with wine.
This is what your Sovereign Lord says, your God, who defends his
people: "See, I have taken out of your hand the cup that made you
stagger; from that cup, the goblet of my wrath, you will never drink
again. I will put it into the hands of your tormentors, who said to you,
'Fall prostrate that we may walk on you.' And you made your back
like the ground, like a street to be walked on."
— Isaiah 51:21-23, NIV

I thank You, Lord, my defender for another victorious day.

By your mighty arm I declare the termination of every affliction and oppression which has interfered with Your plans and purpose for my life.

May every tormenter of my life drink of the cup of Your fury which You have transferred into their hands, may they stumble, stagger, reel, and totally fail in their evil designs against me today, in Jesus' mighty name.

I am free by the blood of Jesus, and no oppressor will ever walk over me again, in Jesus' name, amen.

Day 30

"So then faith comes by hearing, and hearing by the word of God."
— Romans 10:17

I worship You, Father, for another day in Your presence, I thank You for all Your benefits in my life.

O Lord, give me a word tailored to my point of need today. Holy Spirit, let my ears be open to hear Your Word of God to increase my faith. I block my ears from every faith reducing voice, in Jesus' name.

O Lord, put an outstanding praise report in my mouth today, let my life be a testimony of Your mercy, in Jesus' name, amen.

Day 31

"Being confident of this very thing, that He who has begun a good work
in you will complete it until the day of Jesus Christ."
— Philippians 1:6

Thank You, Lord, for the good work you have begun in my life.

As the Bible says, I believe you will complete that good work in Jesus name. I nullify every demonic pronouncement to interrupt your work in my life, I cancel it in Jesus name. I declare, in the name of Jesus Christ, that no voice shall have authority over my life contrary to what You have ordained.

In the mighty name of Jesus, I call forth the quick completion of every divine activity in my life (mention any specific work that comes to mind). This is my day of completion, by the power of the living God, amen.

Day 32

"Who has spoken and it came to pass, unless the Lord has commanded it?" – Lamentations 3:37, ESV

Thank You, Lord, for bringing me safely to another day.

According to the Word, I nullify every pronouncement concerning me, my life, or anything that concerns me which is contrary to divine command. I declare, in the name of Jesus Christ, that no voice shall have authority over my life contrary to what the Lord has ordained. I cancel every word of sickness, bondage, poverty, failure, or sudden disaster, in Jesus' name.

In the mighty name of Jesus, I call forth the quick manifestation of every divine command, prophesy, or promise made about my life (mention any specific promise that comes to mind). This is my month of breaking forth, by the power of the living God, amen.

Day 33

"I was glad when they said unto me, Let us go into the house of the Lord." – Psalm 122:1, KJV

Thank You Lord for another day to fellowship with brothers and sisters in Christ. In the name of Jesus Christ, I call forth people from every corner of my city into our worship service.

Let the hearts of the people stir with joy and their feet hasten them into the church. I call everyone who has been invited to remember and to come to church, in Jesus' name.

I come against every demonic hindrance that will try to keep the people away from our church today. O Lord, make a way for those experiencing any manner of difficulty to overcome.

I pray all these in Jesus' mighty name, amen.

Day 34

"See, I have this day set thee over the nations and over the kingdoms, to root out, and to pull down, and to destroy, and to throw down, to build, and to plant." – Jeremiah 1:10

Thank You Father, for the authority granted me, in the name of Jesus.

O Lord send Your consuming fire now to locate and permanently destroy every stubborn, persistent, demonic root in or around my body, home, family, workspace, business, church, finances, or any other thing pertaining to me, in the mighty name of Jesus.

I frustrate every demonic manifestation of these ungodly roots in my life today, by the anointing of the Holy Spirit.

I pray all these, in Jesus' mighty name, amen.

Day 35

"See, I have this day set thee over the nations and over the kingdoms, to root out, and to pull down, and to destroy, and to throw down, to build, and to plant." – Jeremiah 1:10, KJV

Thank You Father, for the authority granted me, in the name of Jesus.

O Lord, send Your consuming fire now to locate and permanently destroy every stubborn, persistent, demonic root in or around my body, home, family, workspace, business, church, finances, or any other thing pertaining to me, in the mighty name of Jesus.

I frustrate every demonic manifestation of these ungodly roots in my life today by the anointing of the Holy Spirit.

I plant the seeds of goodness, love, mercy, peace, abundance, restoration, and refreshing to replace every ungodly seed, in Jesus mighty name.

I pray all these in Jesus' mighty name, amen.

Notes

Day 36

"See, I have this day set thee over the nations and over the kingdoms, to root out, and to pull down, and to destroy, and to throw down, to build, and to plant." — Jeremiah 1:10, KJV

I come against any and every demonic affliction planted in my body, by curses, incantation, enchantment, genes, sinful activity, witchcraft, and so forth. I pull them out by their roots and cast them into the lake of fire reserved for Satan and his angels.

I plant the seeds of restoration and rebuilding. By Your creative miracle, Lord, repair any losses or damage caused by those destroyed demonic roots, in Jesus' name.

Day 37

"See, I have this day set thee over the nations and over the kingdoms, to root out, and to pull down, and to destroy, and to throw down, to build, and to plant." – Jeremiah 1:10, KJV

I worship You, Lord, I praise Your holy name.

Thank You, Lord, for the authority to build and plant, given to me in Your Word.

In the mighty name of Jesus, I declare a creative miracle of restoration over my body, business, family, church, finances, prayer life, and so forth.

In the name of Jesus, I command the reversal of every loss or damage caused by the destroyed demonic roots.

I speak rebuilding, gains, restoration, vigor, power, boldness, peace, promotion, alertness, health, and increase over my life today, in Jesus' name, amen.

Day 38

"For though we walk in the flesh, we are not waging war according to the flesh. For the weapons of our warfare are not of the flesh but have divine power to destroy strongholds. We destroy arguments and every lofty opinion raised against the knowledge of God, and take every thought captive to obey Christ." – 2 Corinthians 10:3-5, ESV

Lord, open my eyes, deliver me from spiritual ignorance, in Jesus' name, translate me by Your spirit from the realm of physical warfare to that of the spirit, in Jesus' name.

Teach me to war in the spirit, train my hands for battle, Lord, strengthen me to stand against every challenge facing me today, in Jesus' name.

Day 39

"Surely you will summon nations you know not,
and nations you do not know will come running to you, because of the
Lord your God,
the Holy One of Israel, for he has endowed you with splendor."
— Isaiah 55:5, NIV

I am endowed with splendor by the Holy One of Israel.

I summon new contacts and connections to my business, work, and life today. I command them to hasten their steps towards me, in Jesus' name.

I call new people into my church today, I summon people in need of salvation to cross my path as I go about my usual activities. I call them from the east, west, north, and south of my city, in Jesus' name.

I command every reproach over my life to yield to divine splendor, in Jesus' name.

I rebuke every spirit of rejection and shame causing hatred, failure, loss, and pain in my life, I command you to lose your grip and hold over me, in Jesus' mighty name.

Day 40

"And they said, believe on the Lord Jesus Christ, and thou shalt be saved, and thy house." – Acts 16:31, KJV

Thank You, Father, for Your saving grace and for the precious blood of Jesus which was shed for me.

Today, I present every unsaved member of my family (call any specific person by name) before You, Lord, I pray that they will receive the Gospel, in Jesus' name.

Father, I ask that You send a laborer to (name) to win him/her to Christ.

I come against every spiritual blindness and resistance to the Gospel empowered by the god of this age. Release my family and let them go, in Jesus' mighty name, amen.

Day 41

"But Jesus beheld them, and said unto them, with men this is
impossible; but with God all things are possible."
— Matthew 19:26, KJV

I bless You, Lord, for the dawn of a new day.

I yield every difficult, troublesome, or worrying situation into Your hand
O Lord. I command every impossible situation (name the situations) in
my life today to submit to the authority of the Word of God. I declare
a complete turnaround, in Jesus' mighty name.

As I step out to attempt things I have previously attempted without
success, I call forth divine favor to work for me, in Jesus' name.

Today, nothing shall be impossible for me by the anointing of the Holy
Spirit, in Jesus' name, amen.

Day 42

"But Jesus beheld them, and said unto them, With men this is impossible; but with God all things are possible."
– Matthew 19:26, KJV

Lord, open my eyes today to see possibilities instead of impossibilities.

Holy Spirit, transform my heart to a heart of faith instead of doubt. Help me access the level of seeing in the Spirit and believing to take steps of faith today, in Jesus' name.

Lord give me boldness to step into every divine door of opportunity open before me today, in Jesus' name.

Notes

Vivian Ojieh

Day 43

"And it shall come to pass in the last days, saith God, I will pour out of my Spirit upon all flesh: and your sons and your daughters shall prophesy, and your young men shall see visions, and your old men shall dream dreams." – Acts 2:17, KJV

Thank You, Lord, for another opportunity to fellowship in Your house.

O Lord, let Your spirit which has been poured out on all flesh manifest in our church today.

I come against spiritual blindness, apathy, and deafness to God's voice. Loose your hold over the people, in Jesus' mighty name.

In the name of Jesus, I declare today that we will see visions in the spirit as God intends and we will not be worldly minded or desire material gain, but our hearts will desire spiritual gain. Amen.

Day 44

"Open my eyes, that I may behold wondrous things out of your law."
– Psalm 119:18, ESV

Stir in me the desire and longing for Your Word, O Lord. Guide me into Your deep treasures of divine wisdom. Give me understanding as I study, O Lord, unveil Your hidden secrets by the inspiration of Your Holy Spirit in me.

Open my ears also to hear Your Word for my life today, may my spiritual eyes be open to see Your move, in Jesus' name.

Day 45

"See, I have this day set thee over the nations and over the kingdoms, to root out, and to pull down, and to destroy, and to throw down, to build, and to plant." – Jeremiah 1:10, KJV

I worship You, Lord, I praise Your holy name.

Thank You, Lord, for the authority to build and plant given me in Your Word.

In the mighty name of Jesus, I declare a creative miracle of restoration over my body, business, family, church, finances, prayer life, and so forth.

In the name of Jesus, I command the reversal of every loss or damage caused by any demonic roots in or around me.

I speak rebuilding, gains, restoration, vigor, power, boldness, peace, promotion, alertness, health, and increase over my life today, in Jesus' name, amen.

Day 46

"The Spirit of the Lord shall rest upon Him, The Spirit of wisdom and understanding, The Spirit of counsel and might, The Spirit of knowledge and of the fear of the Lord."
— Isaiah 11:2

Thank You, Holy Spirit, for resting permanently with me (this applies to born-again believers in Christ Jesus).

I pray in the name of Jesus, that the anointing for wisdom and understanding, discernment, and discrimination between right and wrong manifest through me today.

O Lord, guide my every decision and action, give me supernatural access to Your deep things, and may I have the fear of the Lord in all I do today, in Jesus' name.

I claim good success in all I do today as I completely submit to the Spirit of God, in Jesus' mighty name, I pray, amen.

Day 47

"Death and life are in the power of the tongue, And those who love it will eat its fruit." – Proverbs 18:21

Thank You, Father, for my tongue of faith and power.

I command this day to align with God's plan and purpose for my life, doors of opportunity and favor shall be open before me, in Jesus' name.

In the name of Jesus, I bind every demonic resistance in the atmosphere, I declare this day shall yield every divine allocation due me, I command the day to manifest my blessings and answered prayers, in Jesus' mighty name.

I speak life to this day, there shall be no loss or death in or around me today, in Jesus' name, amen.

Day 48

"But I am afraid that just as Eve was deceived by the serpent's cunning, your minds may somehow be led astray from your sincere and pure devotion to Christ." – 2 Corinthians 11:3, NIV

Thank You, Lord, for a great new day.

I come against every spirit of deception that will try to separate me from my divine purpose today, in Jesus' name.

I cover my mind with the blood of Jesus. I command you, mind, to align with the Word of Truth instead of the lies of Satan, in Jesus' name.

In the name of Jesus, I break every chain of deception pulling me away from sincere and pure devotion to Christ.

I belong to Jesus! Amen.

Day 49

"'Though the mountains be shaken and the hills be removed, yet my unfailing love for you will not be shaken nor my covenant of peace be removed,' says the Lord, who has compassion on you."
— Isaiah 54:10, NIV

I praise You, Lord, who has rescued me time after time.

I lift all those in a storm's path before You, Lord. Let Your unfailing love and deliverance manifest in the land, let Your mighty hand go forth to intervene in the difficult areas, in the mighty name of Jesus.

Dangerous weather, be still and surrender your force to the power of the Holy Ghost, in Jesus' name.

I come against every blood sucking demon that tries to kill large numbers of people through natural disasters. I come against every paralyzing spirit of fear and terror, in Jesus' name.

O Lord, let Your unfailing love and peace prevail over the shaking mountains, and other structures, in Jesus' name I pray, amen.

Notes

Day 50

"God brings them out of Egypt; He has strength like a wild ox. For there is no sorcery against Jacob, Nor any divination against Israel. It now must be said of Jacob And of Israel, 'Oh, what God has done!'" – Numbers 23:22-23

I thank You, Lord, for bringing me out of every captivity, in Jesus' name. Thank You for the blood of Jesus which was shed for me.

According to Your Word, Lord, I declare today there is no enchantment or divination against me.

By the blood of Jesus, I nullify and completely cancel every word of incantation being said against me, every curse or evil declaration against me, my life, family, business, work, or anything that pertains to me is nullified, in Jesus' name.

In the mighty name of Jesus, I send the Holy Ghost fire to scatter every demonic gathering where my name is being mentioned for evil, and I send their curses like arrows back to them. In Jesus' name, they will eat the fruit of their own words.

Today I am not weak, I have strength like a wild ox.

Day 51

"Then out of them shall proceed thanksgiving And the voice of those who make merry; I will multiply them, and they shall not diminish; I will also glorify them, and they shall not be small." — Jeremiah 30:19

O Lord, fill my mouth with songs of thanks today, let my voice sing happy songs from deep in my spirit.

By the blood of Jesus, I cast off every garment of heaviness, let Your joy manifest and radiate through me everywhere I go today, let someone's life be brightened because of my joy.

In the mighty name of Jesus, I send the Holy Ghost fire against every spirit of loss and scattering. Every good thing I touch today will multiply and increase, in Jesus' name.

As Your glory covers me today, I will shine and be bigger, I will not be small or diminished before my adversaries, in Jesus' name.

Day 52

"Beloved, do not believe every spirit, but test the spirits, whether they are of God; because many false prophets have gone out into the world."
— 1 John 4:1

Holy Spirit, I yield myself completely to You today, sharpen my sense of discernment, in Jesus' name.

As I go about my life, work, or business today, may I not be foolish or naive but wise and able to separate truth from lies, by Your mighty power.

Lord, activate in me the ability to test the spirits of men. Today, I block and reject every false teaching, every false prophecy, and every false counsel. I will hear and receive the voice of Jesus alone, amen.

Day 53

"And this I pray, that your love may abound still more and more in knowledge and all discernment." – Philippians 1:9

Thank You, dear Lord, I worship and adore You, You alone are worthy.

O Lord, let my love grow more in knowledge and all discernment, in Jesus' name.

Holy Spirit, I surrender my all to You today, activate in me the spirit of knowledge and discernment. As I go about my business today, Lord, enable me to see beyond the smiles of men. Lord help me access the deep secrets for today, open my eyes to see in the spirit.

In the name of Jesus, I receive the keys for my spiritual, mental, social, emotional, physical, and financial breakthrough today.

Day 54

"Then Daniel went to his house and made the matter known to
Hananiah, Mishael, and Azariah, his companions."
– Daniel 2:17, ESV

O Lord, raise me committed and like-minded prayer partners who will connect with the same spiritual goal, and who will desire my progress as I desire theirs.

Open my eyes Lord, to identify my prayer partners, and open my spirit to embrace them, in Jesus' name, amen.

Day 55

"Now the Spirit expressly says that in latter times some will depart from the faith, giving heed to deceiving spirits and doctrines of demons."
— 1 Timothy 4:1

Thank You, Jesus, for the sending the Holy Spirit, our comforter, teacher, and friend.

Lord I lift myself before You today, keep me in the true faith by the power of Your Spirit, in Jesus' name.

I pray for anyone the enemy is trying to pull away from the faith (mention anyone who comes to mind), Holy Spirit, hold them back, in Jesus' name.

By Your mighty power, O Lord, I push back and scatter by fire, every deceiving spirit and demonic doctrine from my family, church, city, and environment, in Jesus' name, amen.

Day 56

"Therefore, submit to God. Resist the devil and he will flee from you."
— James 4:7

Thank You, Alpha and Omega, I bless Your holy name.

I lay everything at Your feet, O Lord, I submit my greed, my plans, my ambitions, and my desires to You, I surrender my all to You, Jesus.

Lord, I repent of every stubbornness and resistance to Your voice and authority, I repent of every resistance to the move of Your Holy Spirit in my life, I repent of every disobedience to Your Word and instruction, in Jesus' name.

Today, I resist you, Satan, and all your works of stealing, killing, and destroying. I command you to flee and lose your grip over anything related to me, in Jesus' mighty name, amen.

Notes

Day 57

"Draw near to God and He will draw near to you. Cleanse your hands, you sinners; and purify your hearts, you double-minded."
– James 4:8

Thank You, Father, for Your new mercies.

Lord, I fix my eyes on You today, help me draw near to You by Your spirit. Strengthen me Lord, to cut off from all distractions and everything attempting to take me from Your presence today, in Jesus' name.

Cleanse my hands and heart with the washing of the blood of Jesus, sanctify me, O Lord. As I pray and worship today, let my faith be built up. I dismantle every stronghold of doubt and double-mindedness, in Jesus' name, amen.

Day 58

"But they who wait for the Lord shall renew their strength;
they shall mount up with wings like eagles;
they shall run and not be weary;
they shall walk and not faint." – Isaiah 40:31, ESV

As I wait upon You, Lord, let my spiritual and physical strength be renewed. Use me today to defy natural laws and to manifest the laws of faith, in Jesus' name.

O Lord, amplify my spiritual stamina, that I will be able to continue in prayer without ceasing until I see the manifestation and establishment of Your divine response, in Jesus' mighty name, amen.

Day 59

"But solid food is for the mature, for those who have their powers of discernment trained by constant practice to distinguish good from evil."
— Hebrews 5:14, ESV

I worship You, Lord, there is no one like You. Thank You for the gift of life.

Holy Spirit, activate in me a greater desire for the solid food of Your Word, as the deer pants for the waters, may my soul long for You today, O Lord.

Train me, Lord, mold me, act in me to become more spiritually mature today, in Jesus' name. Holy Spirit, my teacher, create opportunities to train my powers of discernment today, in Jesus' name.

As I go about my business today, as I make decisions and choices, help me discern between good and evil, in Jesus' mighty name, amen.

Day 60

"Immediately he made the disciples get into the boat and go before him to the other side, while he dismissed the crowds. And after he had dismissed the crowds, he went up on the mountain by himself to pray. When evening came, he was there alone."
– Matthew 14: 22-23, ESV

Draw me close today, Holy Spirit, as I separate myself from the crowds and draw near to You. Lord, guide me. Let me hear Your voice and see You move, in Jesus' name.

O Lord, increase my sensitivity in the spirit, let me discern when to shift from the natural into the supernatural.

Notes

Scripture Index

Vivian Ojieh

www.ingramcontent.com/pod-product-compliance
Lightning Source LLC
Chambersburg PA
CBHW020558030426
42337CB00013B/1136